Beautiful & Majestic Flowers

Coloring Book

_____

Jose Valladares

CSP Publishing

This edition published in 2021 by Circlesquare Projections

Copyright© by Circlesquare Projections

ISBN: 978-0-578-86429-7

Circlesquare Projections Publishing company
Pacoima, Los Angeles, CA, 91331

Table of Contents

Introduction

This new coloring book is about having fun, and releasing stress. Being stress free takes effort and commitment. You will color 81 beautiful and majestic designs, and you'll need to buy some colored pencils, markers or gel pens. I have included one design per page to color the pages with ease.

Coloring book supplies:

- Crayola colored pencils or Prismacolor premier colored pencils

- Blending pencils - helps you blend colors together

- Pencil sharpener

- Brush tip markers

- A storage bin to stored all your supplies

Coloring flowers is easy and fun, and I hope you enjoy coloring these designs as much as I do.

Have fun!

Princess Alyssum

Lavatera

Sweet sweet love

Passionate sweetness

Mandala flower

Cotton Candy

Pink Celebration

I miss you

Scarlet sage

Two fishes

Eternal love

Beautiful & Majestic Flowers Coloring Book   **35**

My strawberries

Peace & love

Fake flowers

Classic rose

Peaceful rose

Queen of the meadow

Garden statue

Warm sunset

Sacred geometry petals

Moon flower

Peaceful gardener

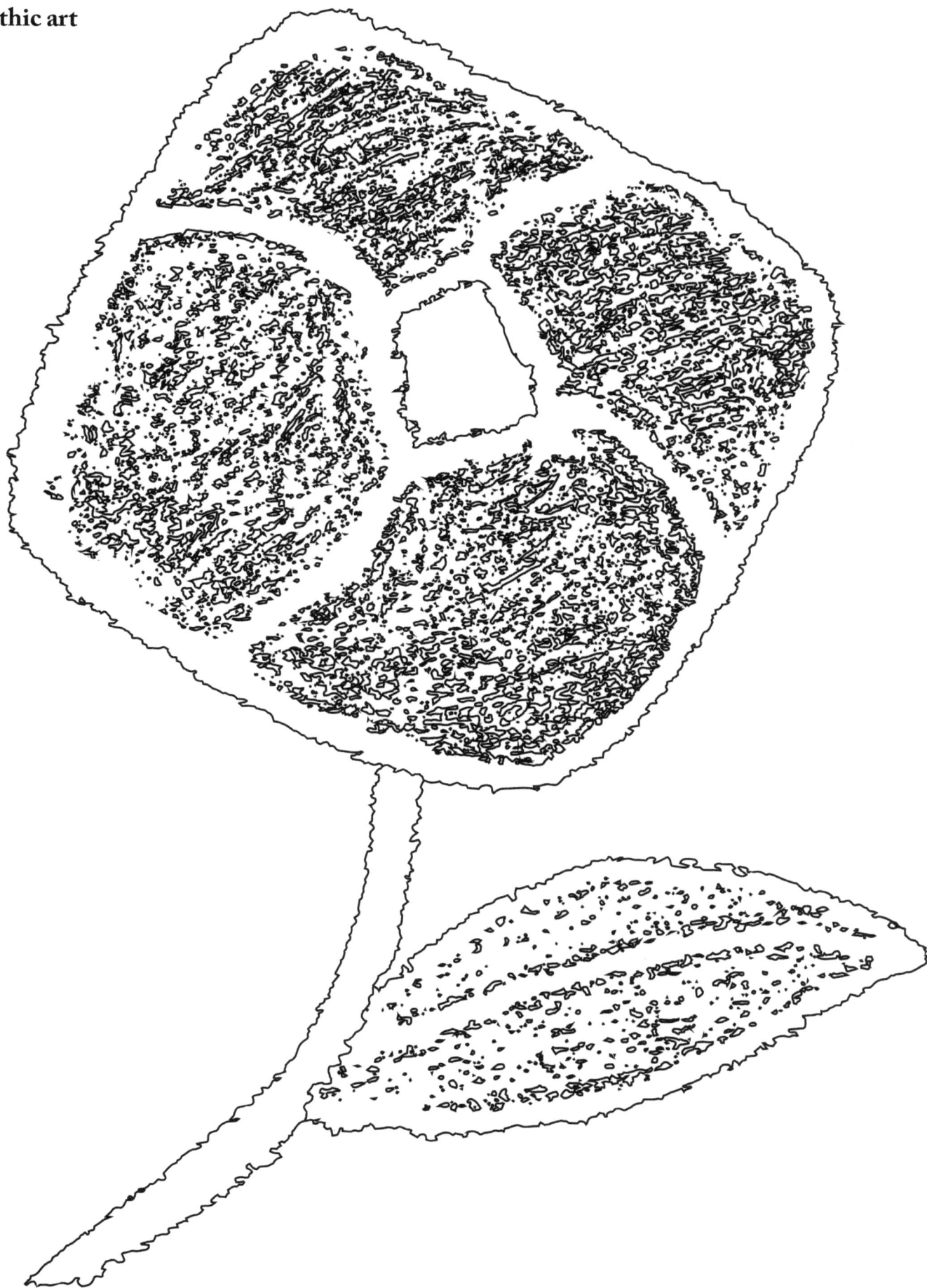

Rose of sharon

Peaceful love

Sleepy flower

Tickseed

Morning glory

Blooming love

Elegant rose

Green leaves

Love pup

Digital flower

Endless romance bouquet

Elephants in love

Rosa rubiginosa

Platonic solid flower

Radiant devotion

Key to the heart

98

Wedelia

Purple rose

Bird house

Water hyacinth

For sweetheart

Daydream bouquet

Peaceful primula

Sweet friendship

Valentine flower

Flower in wax

Paster passion

Spring wisteria

Wild rose

Be happy

Revolutionary flor

Lovely carnations

Heart & soul

Birds in love

Dance of love

Surprise!

Circle of life

Ultimate elegance

Leucanthemum

Summer leaf

Lilac family

Flowery clouds

Singing bird

Village

Persian flower

Acknowledgement

Some images have been designed using resources from freepik.com

Some images have been designed using resources from pexels.com

Some images have been designed using resources from embcart.com

About the Author:

Every month, I get a regular source of income from supporters who've pledged to me through Patreon. Having their ongoing support means I spend less time thinking about business, and more time creating.

Check out all my published material:

amazon.com/author/josevalladares
https://www.patreon.com/circlesquare777